Marketing

Mastery

Workbook

By

Amanda Rose

Clarity

One of the most important questions you need to ask yourself is, "What am I trying to say?" What's your message? What is the point of what you're trying to say? It should be easy for us to understand your message.

Every communication should have 1 main point to make. As soon as we get into trying to discuss multiple points, we lose our audience. It gets convoluted and confusing. Keep it simple. Keep a separate point for a separate message.

In addition to having a single main point to each post on social media, what is your overall message? What is the change you are aiming to create? How are you helping your audience? Are you keeping your posts on theme? If your business is about meditation and you're posting about water skiing, does it connect, or are you off-theme?

Take a look at your current posts...
Do I have a single message, or am I often trying to make multiple points? _____

_____

_____

Is my message clear and concise, or is it a little confusing to someone just tuning in? _____

_____

_____

Do I have clarity on my overall theme or message that carries through in all of my messages? _____

_____

_____

_____

_____

_____

_____

How can I improve on the clarity of my message? ___

_____

_____

_____

_____

_____

_____

_____

_____

_____

_____

_____

_____

Brand

What is a brand? The term often seems ambiguous, so let's simplify and clarify it.

A Brand is:
How we recognize a business or product

That's all it boils down to. Recognition. So, how do we recognize a brand at a glance?

- Color Scheme
- Slogans/Tag Lines
- Writing Style
- Images
- Logos

These elements combine to craft a brand. When your audience is scrolling on social media they should be able to immediately know it's your post without looking at your name just by the look, feel, and style of it.

My 1-2 Primary Brand Colors are: _____

_____

_____

_____

My 2-4 Accent Brand Colors are: _____

_____

_____

_____

My Slogan/Tag-Line is: _____

_____

_____

_____

My Writing Style is: _____

_____

_____

_____

My Imagery is: _____

_____

_____

_____

My Logo is: _____

_____

_____

_____

Niche

Who is your ideal client? This is crucial to determine. The more specific you are, the more defied this person is, the easier you'll find it to market.

Why? Because you'll know their wants, needs, hopes, desires, struggles, hobbies, etc. You are talking to someone specific, and when you speak to someone directly they will go, "Wow! They're talking directly to me!" And this is how you build the initial relationship and foster trust.

Who are you serving? Let's get clear on this:

My Niche Market Is...

My Ideal Client Demographic is: _____

_____

_____

_____

_____

_____

My Ideal Client Enjoys These Hobbies in Their Spare Time: _____

_____

_____

_____

_____

_____

My Ideal Client Struggles With: _____

_____

_____

_____

_____

My Ideal Client Wants: _____

_____

_____

_____

_____

My Ideal Client Gets Excited About: _____

_____

_____

_____

_____

_____

My Ideal Clients Goals Are: _____

_____

_____

_____

_____

_____

My Ideal Clients Responds best to: _____

_____

_____

_____

_____

_____

To help you make these determinations, here are some questions you can ask about your ideal client:

How old are they?
Are they single or married?
Where do they live?
Do they rent or own their home?
What's most important to them?
What fears do they have?
Are they an introvert or extravert?
Are they parents, want to be parents, or don't want kids?
Do they have a job?
What do they like to spend their time doing?
What are their aspirations?
What do they have a hard time with?
Are they serious?
Do they have a sense of humor?
Are they a perfectionist?
Have they started working on their dream yet?
Are the more visual, audio, or kinesthetic?

As you can see, asking these types of questions can help you gain deep insight into the person you're talking to. This takes your message from ambiguity into a defined message that is meaningful to your niche. Keep asking questions and get really clear on who this individual is.

Unique Selling Proposition

Essential the USP is what sets your product and you apart from everything and everyone else. First you will want to determine your unique factors, and secondly, you'll want to compile a 2-5 sentence way of communicating that.

This will answer the two main questions a potential client has, which are, "Why should I buy *your* product?" and, "Why should I buy it from *you?*"

What Makes You Unique? _____

_____

_____

_____

_____

What Makes Your Product or Service Unique? _____

_____

_____

_____

_____

Sample Unique Selling Proposition for a Service:

Hello, my name is Jane Doe, and I am a business coach for experienced online service-based entrepreneurs who are stuck at 1-5K months and who want to start generating 10K+ months. I am the only coach who uses the XYZ method which utilizes a variety of mindset techniques that integrate the mind-body connection. My systematic approach is different from the traditional business coach, in that we use XYZ to create lasting change on a cellular level.

Sample Unique Selling Proposition for a Product:

Hi, my name is John Doe, and I'm the creator of the XYZ glasses. I was an optometrist for 10 years and in that time, I developed a passion for eyewear after seeing the struggles of my clients to find glasses that gave them confidence. These XYZ glasses are the first to incorporate dynamic adaption to eye-distance, while simultaneously being aesthetically designed by the leading eyewear designers in Paris. We are the exclusive designers for unique eyewear used in the latest films produced by ZYX Studios.

These statements need to have a wow factor. The words *unique, only, exclusive, single, different, rare, etc.* are words that POP in a USP.

Now it's time to write your own USP:

_____

_____

_____

_____

_____

_____

_____

_____

_____

_____

_____

_____

Elevator Pitch

A 1-3 sentence pitch for your product of service. This gets us down to the essence, the essentials, of what you offer. You should be able to explain what your product or service is and what is does.

You'll use elevator pitches for your overall business, for every product you create, for every service; it's very important to get good at explaining your products and services in a clear and concise way.

Let's review some examples:

FIRE FURY FREEDOM Elevator Pitch

"Fire Fury Freedom is a sci-fi dystopian novel with a splash of fantasy. It takes place on a world where global warming has hit its apex, a mega-corporation has taken over as government, and a renegade mercenary group sets out on a quest to save the world. This is the type of book that takes you on and adventure and makes the rest of the world fade away."

COURSE CREATION Elevator Pitch

"The Course Creation 5-Day Complete Course Builder Workshop is a complete step-by-step guide to creating an online course. This covers everything from how to pick a topic, to formatting, content creation, how to market and sell it, and the #1 secret to course creation that 95% of entrepreneurs get wrong. This will give you everything you need to create online courses with ease and sell them with confidence."

Formatting:

1. Introduce Yourself, Your Company, and/or Your Product
2. Tell us about it, give us the story, get us engaged
3. Why should they take action / What will they get out of it if they take action?

Keep is simple, engaging, and exciting. Elevator pitches should never be dull; they are meant to inspire. Always remember that people take action based on emotion, not rationale.

My Elevator Pitch

_____

_____

_____

_____

_____

_____

_____

_____

_____

_____

_____

_____

_____

_____

Mission Statement

A short, most often 8-20-word statement, that explains what the mission of your business is. This is a clear, direct, and concise statement that serves to inspire and motivate. Often this tells us who you serve and what you hope to accomplish as your overall goal.

Examples:

Best Friends Animal Society
"A better world through kindness to animals."

Amanda Rose Coaching
"Shifting human consciousness to create soulful abundance through mindset practices."

Nordstrom
"To give customers the most compelling shopping experience possible."

Life is Good
"To spread the power of optimism."

This is essentially very simple. This is the change you want your company to impact the world with. This is the 'why,' the fuel to the fire, the inspiration that gets you excited to show up every day. What is the impact you want to create?

My Mission Statement

_____

_____

_____

_____

_____

_____

Authenticity

We hear about authenticity a lot. "Be you, be authentic," but... what does that *really* mean? When you're trying to figure out social media marketing it's very common to start following success social media marketers. While, yes, we can learn a lot from following them, we can also get stuck in comparing ourselves to them or fall into the 'copycat' trap.

The 'copycat' trap is when we start to mimic them. We start to copy their writing style, trying to mimic their photos, and basically play pretend. While this may have short-term gains, overall, it's not the strategy you want to use.

Being authentic means to be genuine; this means embracing who you are, your likes, dislikes, opinions, experiences, struggles, successes, and sharing from this place of open honesty. This is what makes you unique. This is what makes you relatable. This is what will make your ideal clients love you, and what will repel the people who aren't in alignment with you. It's the repelling aspect that scares most people.

Why? Because we all want to be liked. We don't want people to dislike us. This fear holds most people back from speaking from their own voice.

In defining yourself, your business, your message, and your brand, it takes bravely saying, "this is who I am!" Let the people who don't resonate with you leave so you can make room for the people who will love you and be inspired by you!

Self-Acceptance

If you've felt fear or doubt about speaking from your heart, your first step is self-acceptance. You need to be head-over-heels in love with the amazing person YOU are! Whether you struggle with this or not, I want you to reinforce this. We're going to get empowered and inspired about ourselves!

10 Things I love About Me Are:

1. _____

2. _____

3. _____

4. _____

5. _____

6. _____

7. _____

8. _____

9. _____

10. _____

Amanda Rose

10 Unique Things About Me Are

1. _____
2. _____
3. _____
4. _____
5. _____
6. _____
7. _____
8. _____
9. _____
10. _____

My Favorite Color is _____

My Favorite Movie is _____

My Favorite Quote is _____

My favorite Pass times Are _____

_____

_____

I'm told people like my _____

_____

I Feel Strongly About _____

_____

_____

_____

_____

I want to inspire people to _____

_____

_____

_____

_____

I Like to Talk About _____

_____

_____

_____

Everything you just wrote about, everything you just said, is your authentic self. It's your voice. It's your passions. Did you know that the #1 people search about celebrities is what they wear to the grocery store? It might sound odd, but here's the thing; people are trying to find a connection. They want to bridge the gap. They want to feel like your real person they can get to know. So be brave and be you.

Get a cyber bully? Block 'em. Think about your favorite celebrity; someone who has deeply inspired you. Imagine if they stopped because of one of their bullies (and trust me, they have had MANY). You wouldn't have had the opportunity to have been influenced by their gifts if they had let the bullies discourage them. This is the same for you. You're going to inspire countless people by bravely being you, ignore the bullies so you message can reach the people who need it!

Vulnerability

Vulnerability translates into relatability. If you're always portraying yourself as having everything perfectly done, that everything is sunshine and rainbows in your life, then your audience will feel divided from you. Why? Because they struggle, and if they don't see your struggle, they won't be able to relate to you.

Now, and I can't stress this enough:

NEVER: Use vulnerability for vulnerabilities sake

ALWAYS: Use vulnerability with a purpose

What does this mean? Vulnerability for vulnerabilities sake along means sharing your struggles bluntly, example:

"Man, today has been a DAY! I've had a headache all day, my internet was down for hours so I couldn't even work, and the kids both got sick! Can't wait for it to be over..."

Does this make you seem more human? Yes. Is it inspiring or helping your audience? No. Does it make you seem like a leader who can help others? No. We see this type of post on social media constantly.

Now let's try the same scenario, but using vulnerability with a purpose:

"Today was not what I expected.

I woke up with a headache...

The internet decided to take a 3-hour break from its job...

And both of my kids have been down and out with tummy bugs...

At first, I felt frustrated, and overwhelmed, and I just couldn't wait for it to be over. As time ticked by I took stock. I remembered what my coach told me about looking for the good in every situation.

I started to look for the silver lining and I began to realize how lucky I am.

I didn't have to ask my boss for a day off since I work for myself now.

I'm already home so taking care of the kiddos wasn't a huge inconvenience.

I set my own hours, so I just moved my schedule around and got my work done when the internet popped back on.

I never used to have this kind of freedom. A few years ago, this would have been a horrible day and to top it off I would have had to have lost a day's pay for taking off from work and had a ton of paperwork to catch up on the following day.

No, not every day is a breeze. Entrepreneur life isn't for everyone, but man alive, I wouldn't trade this for anything."

As you can see we've got the same situation but a completely different spin on it. It's all about the perspective. What is the message? You struggled, but you overcame. Use your struggles to show your audience how you're human, and you have your bad days and your difficulties, but that you overcome or that you have a positive takeaway. That's the path of the leader.

Let's brainstorm a few ideas where you can express vulnerability and overcoming:

Struggle: _____
_____
_____
_____

What you Learned / How you Overcame: _____
_____
_____
_____
_____

Struggle: _____

_____

_____

_____

What you Learned / How you Overcame: _____

_____

_____

_____

Struggle: _____

_____

_____

_____

What you Learned / How you Overcame: _____

_____

_____

_____

Struggle: _____

_____

_____

_____

What you Learned / How you Overcame: _____

_____

_____

_____

Content

We've just explored so many incredible aspects of marketing; and there's a reason we looked at all of that before content, and that's because those elements inspire your content!

It becomes as natural as breathing to create content when we know who we're talking to, when we're clear about who we are, when we're willing to be vulnerable, and when we know our mission. What creates mental barriers when it comes to content creation is overthinking and uncertainty.

Use your content to inspire and educate. You want to impart value to your audience. When you constantly provide valuable content, you will foster trust and give your followers a reason to stay around, and eventually, to buy from you when you present an offer.

While overall, with a solid understanding of your ideal clients wants, needs, and struggles, as well as taking the leap to speaking authentically and sharing your journey, for those 'writers-block days' where you need some inspiration, let's create a topics list to come back to...

Content Creation Inspiration

Things that My Target Audience Enjoys

1.

2.

3.

4.

5.

6.

7.

Topics My Ideal Client Likes to read About

1.

2.

3.

4.

5.

6.

7.

Knowledge I Can Impart

1.

2.

3.

4.

5.

6.

7.

Struggles I've Overcome

1.

2.

3.

4.

5.

6.

7.

Inspiration

1.

2.

3.

4.

5.

6.

7.

Self-discovery I Can Share

1.

2.

3.

4.

5.

6.

7.

Other topics around me, my clients, and my business

1.

2.

3.

4.

5.

6.

7.

8.

9.

10.

11.

12.

13.

14.

15.

16.

17.

18.

19.

20.

21.

22.

23.

24.

BONUS: Within 3 Scrolls...

Part of marketing in the social media space includes making it clear who you are and what your message is at any given time to anyone who finds your page. This includes your personal page and your businesses page(s).

When you are building a business, you believe in it is part of who you are. You are making a positive impact in this world; making that clear on your personal space is important. It's equally important to bring your human nature to your business page to allow your brand to be personable and approachable.

So, within three scrolls on any of your pages at any given time, I should know...

- Who You Are
- What your Business Is
- What Your Message Is

Your page should utilize your brand in its images and colors. Utilize the ability to link up your groups, websites, and other social media platforms. Use the "About Me" space to share your mission statement.

Keep this three-scroll rule of thumb in mind. Every so often go to one of your pages and scroll three times. See what you see. Is it clear who you are and what you do? If yes, keep it up, if not make some changes.

A Few of Amanda's Other Courses...

Master your mindset and you master your life! The key to success, wealth, happiness, health, and all of the good things you WANT in your life are unlocked through your mindset!

In this special 90-Minute Mastermind I will teach you...

🌙 How your thoughts have been dictating your results

🌙 Why mastering your mindset is the key to your success

🌙 Why you are where you are based on your past conditioning

🌙 How to reprogram your mind to support you in creating the life you've always wanted

🌙 How to retrain your mind to support you instead of hinder you

🌙 How you can have MORE fun and make MORE money while you Work LESS

🌙 And much more...

A 90-Minute session with me would normally cost $375, but for this Mindset Mastery 90-Minute Mastermind you're going to get in for JUST $11!!!

Contact Amanda to Gain Access Amanda@AmandaRoseFitness.com

This is a 5-Day workshop that will take you through everything from how to choose your topic, structure your course, create content, and how to market and sell it!

In 5-Days You'll have ALL of the skills you need to create and launch your course!

You're going to get...

✨ The #1 Insider Secret to Creating a Course that Sells VS one That Flops

✨ Step-By-Step walk-through on creating your course from concept to launch

✨ Daily Video Training

✨ Daily Written Training

✨ 1:1 Messenger and Voice Message Access to Amanda for Individual Help

✨ Launch Strategies

✨ Course Creation Workbook PDF

Are you ready to create your course, help others learn, and expand your biz?! Let's do this!

This 5-Day workshop is just $222. Register Here:
https://amanda-rose.mykajabi.com/offers/RLeeQAhF

Money Mastery
90 Minute
Mastermind

In the Money Mastery 90-Minute Mindset Gurus, Xerces A Lewis Your Intuitive Soul Doctor, and Amanda Rose Mindset Coach & Author of the Manifesting Series will help you...

💰 To heal your relationship with money so that you naturally begin to attract it

💰 To understand the true meaning of wealth and abundance so that you aren't subconsciously repelling it

💰 Learn what they NEVER taught you in school about wealth creation

💰 Understand how the rich think differently from the poor & the middle class

💰 To get into the energetic flow of money so that you become a money magnet!

95% of wealthy people started with nothing. That means YOU can too!

We're going to show you the path, the only question is... are you ready to walk it?

A 90-Minute session with Myself and Xerces would normally cost $565, but for this Mindset Mastery 90-Minute Mastermind you're going to get in for JUST $88!

Contact Amanda to Gain Access Amanda@AmandaRoseFitness.com

This course is going to cover everything from the writing process, to editing, formatting, and publishing, and how to successfully market your book. what works and how to do it properly, and what to avoid. It's compiling over a year's worth of research, so you don't have to spend endless hours trying to figure out what to do to get your book recognized, in the press, into bookstores, libraries, and land book signings.

If you're ready to finally write your book, get it out in the world, and generate an incredible income through book royalties, then it's time to sign up for this 3-week online workshop!

Learn More:
 https://amanda-rose.mykajabi.com/offers/7bUzKNX2/checkout

About the Author

Amanda Rose is an avid reader and storyteller. Working in a variety of mediums and genres, communicating new ways of thinking is her passion.

Amanda works as an online Health and Fitness coach, Mindset & Business Coach, Actor, Model, Motivational Speaker, Online Course Creator and Writer.

Residing in Kingston, Ontario, with her husband and 3 cats, Amanda is currently working on her next novel. Get in touch with Amanda by visiting her website:

HTTPS://Amanda-rose.mykajabi.com

Manifesting Your Best Life

Manifesting Your Best Life Book Description:

Stop dreaming about a better life and start living it!

Manifesting You Best Life is going to show you that "Living Your Best Life" isn't just some cute meme on social media – it can be your way of life! The 21 nugget-of-wisdom chapters in this self-help book are for people who want to start living their best life, but don't know where to begin. It will give you the skills to take you from dreaming about your best life, to making it your reality!

You will learn:
•How to Identify what living your best life really means to you.
•The steps needed to stop wishing and start living your best life.
•How to use the Law of Attraction to support your efforts.
•Successful habits that will change your life.
•And how to create the life you've always wanted... And start living it NOW!

By the end of Manifesting Your Best Life, you will have a clear picture of what your dream life looks like, how to get there, and the tools and skills to make it into your reality!

Are you ready to begin?

ALSO AVAILABLE ON AUDIBLE

The Manifesting 30-Day Guided Journal

From the author of Manifesting on Purpose comes The Manifesting 30-Day Guided Journal!

This Law of Attraction Based Journal will take your Manifesting Practice to The Next Level!

The Manifesting 30-Day Guided Journal will walk you through 30 days of curated activities that will get you into the energetic flow of manifestation. Through goal-setting, mindfulness, clarity, and actionable steps, you will learn how to create the life of happiness and freedom that you've always desired.

The Orgasmic Cookbook

The Orgasmic Cookbook Book Description:

Nutrition Meets Flavor.

Just because it's healthy doesn't mean it should be boring. In *The Orgasmic Cookbook* Amanda teaches her best tips and tricks to make healthy food pop with flavor! Having lost over 100 pounds Amanda knows the importance of eating healthy. As a food lover she's made it her mission to create healthy recipes packed with rich taste!

Get ready for mouth-watering recipes that will give you a whole new appreciation for food!

Manifesting on Purpose

Manifesting on Purpose Book Description:

It's time to take manifesting off auto-pilot, get behind the wheel, and start steering your life in the direction you want it to go!

Manifesting on Purpose clarifies why we manifest what we do, why we experience the same things over and over again, until we step in and weed out our own mental gardens.

Ever wonder how is it that 2 people can start off with the same opportunity, and one will become a massive success, while the other barely scrapes by? What's the defining factor?

What do successful people know that we're missing? We've been taught that the harder we work the more money, happiness, and success we'll have in life; but if this was the case successful people would constantly we run ragged, and be bleary eyed from lack of sleep, instead of enjoying lots of free time pursuing their heart's desires. So, what are we missing?

The Law of Attraction is always working, even when we're not focused on it. The Law of Attraction states that, "Like Attracts Like," we are all energy, so our thoughts get reflected back to us. Your thoughts create your physical reality. The problem? We're always thinking! Our thoughts, ungoverned, bounce around from idea to idea, and all too often, focus on the immediate problems in our lives, creating a feedback loop. Since we attract back what we think about, if we're focused on our problems, what's going to show up? More problems!

Your mind is your most valuable asset. Your thoughts literally create your reality. Your current situation is a reflection of your previous thoughts. Most people, however, do not consciously decide what they want, their subconscious belief systems run everything on auto-pilot; making most people feel as if they are victims of their circumstances. YOU ARE NOT A VICTIM OF CIRCUMSTANCE!

You are in the driver's seat, you simply have to take control of the wheel! Take manifesting off auto-pilot and create the life you want! "But I think positive thoughts," you say. Your conscious thoughts will always be secondary to your subconscious thoughts in the way of manifestation. Until you change your core beliefs to line up with who you wish to become, and what you wish to do, you cannot break the old cycles.

Are you ready to take control? Have abundance in money, love, health, freedom, experiences, and all other areas of your life? Then let's get started!

Manifesting Money: How to Master and Apply Abundance Mindset in Your Life

Manifesting Money Book description: Master Your Mindset and You Master Your Life!

Why does 99% of the population struggle financially? Is it a lack of opportunity? An issue with education? Not having the right skills? Poor investment choices? Bad timing? Low work performance?

The startling answer is: none of the above!

Wealth creation is a mindset.

It's not what rich people *do*, but how they *think* that sets them apart. *Manifesting Money* is going to teach you how to:

•Discover and Get Rid of Money Blocks

•Kick Fear and Doubt to the Curb

•Create New Supportive Money Beliefs

•Develop Wealth Consciousness

•Build Multiple Sources of Income

•Work Smarter Not Harder

•Manage Money

•Implement the Successful Habits Rich People Use

•Have the Wealth You've Always Wanted

It's time to start *Manifesting Money*!

Get Published Workbook: Write | Publish | Market

Get Published Workbook Book Description:

Most people have thought about publishing a book, but the majority will never even begin writing one. Why? The process can seem daunting. Conceptualizing, writing, editing, formatting, copywriting, publishing, and finally marketing; it can seem like an overwhelming amount of work when you aren't sure what each step entails.

In this workbook, you're going to learn all of my best practices so you can go from concept to published in 2-6 months pending on the length and style of your book, with full knowledge of what to expect, and what to do, so nothing will stand in your way of becoming a successful author!

Self-publishing is an incredible avenue to get your work to your readers fast, with widespread distribution, that allows you to take the lion's share of the profits for the book you put all the work into creating!

With self-publishing, you're in control, but that also means you are in charge of your own marketing campaign. Don't let that scare you away! With social media and online sales booming, you can reach your ideal reader audience easier, and at much less cost, than with traditional marketing. You just need to learn how!

Through this book, you're going to learn...

- How to brainstorm and develop a concept
- How to effectively begin writing your book
- How to create disciplined habits to finish your book
- How to edit, format, and polish your book so it's ready for publication
- Why reviews are the life-blood of self-publishing, and how to get them
- How to write an effective book description
- How to write a gripping back cover
- Why your book cover is your most important investment
- How the self-publishing process works
- Best practices for ultimate exposure
- How to use inexpensive pay-per-click campaigns to drive traffic
- Social Media Marketing
- Free marketing practices
- Inexpensive marketing options
- Importance of an author web site to boost SEO

...And much more!

Fire Fury Freedom

"A veritable saga of a dystopian novel by an author with a genuine flair for detailed originality, and narrative driven storytelling, "Fire Fury Freedom" by Amanda Rose is an extraordinary and truly memorable read from cover to cover." -*Midwest Book Review*

Prequel to the Fire Fury Frontier Series

Fire Fury Freedom Book Description:

A dying planet on the verge of collapse.... tormented pasts that haunt the present... an ancient hidden magick...

The C.D.F.P. mega-corporation rules all, with unchecked power, and dark secrets...

The planet is dying, and they are the last hope to save it... Mack, an ex-soldier of the C.D.F.P. military division, and his mercenaries, standalone against the C.D.F.P. (AKA the Company), in the fight for humanities survival. Left unchallenged, the company has ruled over the East Green Continent with an iron fist for decades. The pollution they've caused has devastated the planet, destroying the ozone, and killing off plant and animal life.

Outside of domed cities the air is thin, and the sun scorches all; it's a veritable wasteland. In the past two decades the planet has reached entirely new levels of decay. Extreme weather patterns, and massive quakes, ravage the land.

Time is running out...

Mack and his mercenary troupe set out on a quest to stop the C.D.F.P. once and for all, and the planet will test them to their limits... But are they ready for the horrors they'll uncover? Can they alone stand up against the all-powerful C.D.F.P.?

Fire Fury Frontier

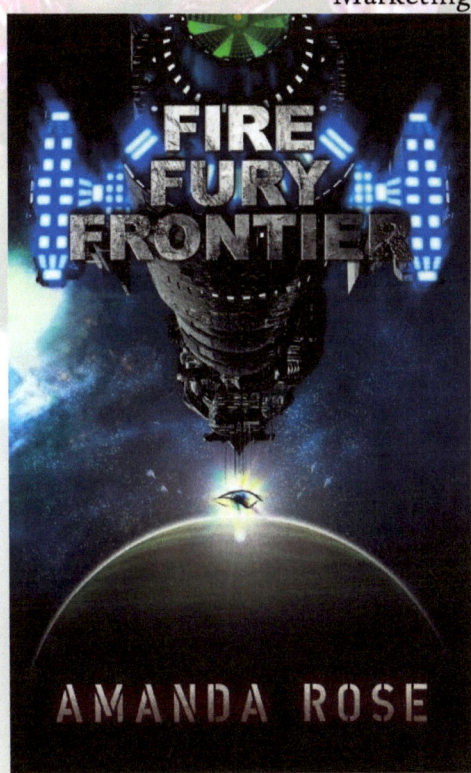

Fire Fury Frontier Book Description:

One ship, one last chance to survive...

Humanity's home world has been destroyed from extensive global warming. For over two hundred years the last remaining humans have lived in space aboard a single massive ship, the Saisei. After generations in space, living aboard a ship is all anyone has ever known.

But space is an inhospitable home.

The ship is old and damaged, rations are low, and a planet fit for colonization has never been found.

In the vast expanse of space, as the Saisei makes way to resupply their ship, they stumble upon a discovery that will change the course of human history forever.

ALSO AVAILABLE ON AUDIBLE

The Impending End

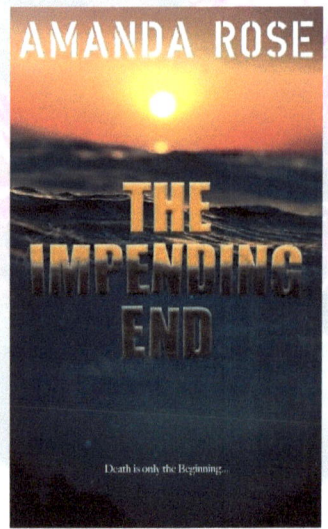

The Impending End Book Description:

It's 2005. Ayla Jefferson is 17, incredibly intelligent, sensitive, imaginative, and thoughtful. She's also contemplating suicide...

After a life long battle with mental illness plaguing her every move, Ayla is ready for death. Eerily calm, she says her goodbyes, and sets out to commit her final act.

But despite her stubborn conviction, life isn't as easy to let go of as she expected. Her hyper-imagination blurs reality and she finds herself getting lost in gripping memories. Mentally disengaged, Ayla's experiences are surreal, and discerning fact from fiction becomes harder and harder.

As the life she's so eager to leave behind begs to hold on, will she be able to leave it all behind?

A Strange Dream: Anthology of Short Stories and Poetry

A Strange Dream Book Description:

Death, Depression, Insomnia, Prostitution, Eating Disorders, Abortion, Convicts, Insanity, and Marital issues... This anthology of short stories and poetry explores the dark reaches of the mind and mental health issues.

The 9 short stories, including award winning EGGS and OUTSIDER, as well as runner up in the Canadian Writer's Guild Short Prose competition, DROWNING IN SILENCE, and 9 poems, take us on a journey from the surreal to the mundane. From day-to-day life to fantasy, the characters and situations explore many walks of life.

www.ingramcontent.com/pod-product-compliance
Lightning Source LLC
Chambersburg PA
CBHW040750200526
45159CB00025B/1832